DAILY Sparkles

Illuminate your Life with 1000 Glimmers

EMMA JASPER

ROCK
POINT

For anyone building a
life full of sparkles

Contents

Introduction

I found glimmers, or "sparkles," as I will be calling them
for this book, at a time when my life could be
described as anything but glimmering: I was
heartbroken, unemployed, selling my home, and
moving back in with my parents.

Nothing was exactly sparkling. Life was hard, and even
though I was familiar with gratitude, I struggled to find
anything to be grateful for. I didn't have it in me. So I
embraced the tiny moments in my day that brought
peace. I began to note what prompted those moments
of calm, and: none of the moments were big. They
were moments easily overlooked without intention:
things like how fresh the first sip of coffee tastes or
how the mug you're drinking from warms your fingers
in the cold. My dog's little bean-paws. How you can
smell the ocean before you can see it. Those
moments—those sparkles—became my lifeline,
calming my nervous system and helping ground me.
When life felt hard, even impossible, those moments

were there. When nothing felt stable, those sparkles were there.

Although my life has gotten distinctly more sparkly, I haven't stopped looking for the sparkles. They remain my greatest tool to help calm anxiety and feel reassured. And the most wonderful part of sparkles is that they're endless. Once you start seeing them, you can't unsee them. Like when you buy a new car and suddenly the roads are full of them. There are a few ways to encourage yourself to see a sparkle, but my favorite way is through nature. Get outside and use your senses: Do you smell a recently mown lawn? Can you hear the birds?

The beautiful thing about sparkles is that you don't need to do anything to find them. You don't need to meditate on them or journal about them. No need to make a list or buy any tools. If it's hard to start, pick something you can see, hear, smell, touch, or taste. Notice any little moment you feel calm and let it add a sparkle to your world.

What Are Glimmers?

Instead of grandiose, expansive experiences, glimmers
are micromoments—subtle yet profound instances
that gently mold our internal landscape. They are the
small miracles and beauties of life that teach our
nervous system the language of safety and calm.
"Glimmers," as coined by the insightful Deb Dana in
her 2018 book *The Polyvagal Theory in Therapy*, are
like delicate sparks of magic in the tapestry of our
existence. But we must first slow down and appreciate
these tender moments when they come.

This book is organized by seasons, allowing you to
discover moments of sparkle throughout the year.
Whether you're seeking daily inspiration or looking to
rediscover peace during challenging times, these
pages will guide you to your personal season of
sparkle. Additionally, there's an "Everyday" chapter
filled with timeless sparkles that can be found no
matter the season.

Spring

The barely-there haze of trees beginning
to bloom.

The first night you sleep with the
windows open as the weather starts
to warm.

Watching a little bird make their nest,
plucking twigs and leaves until it's
just right

The earthy, grounding smell after
a big rain

The fuzzy yellow down of a new
duckling blowing in the warm breeze.

Cozying up on a rainy day with a book under a blanket and with the window cracked open

The first morning you can walk outside without needing a heavy winter jacket.

Waking the garden up after a winter's freeze and making space for spring's blooms

Little ants marching in a line, each with their own mission, somehow knowing what to do and where to go.

The fresh, damp smell of the woods after rain

Fuzzy caterpillars
(Was anybody else obsessed with
finding caterpillars as a kid?)

Discovering a place where you can sit
outside during a rainstorm and stay dry

Birds using birdhouses.

A squirrel eating an acorn with their
cheeks full to bursting.

Noticing a bluebird perched on
your fence

A birdwatching group getting back
together.

The sound of rain on your roof as you lay cuddled up in bed.

A bird taking a bath and flapping their wings like a little dance.

The abundance of bird chirps filling the air.

The way an adorable pup's paws turn grinch green after playing in a wet, freshly mown lawn.

The curious shape of mushrooms

Sprawling green college campuses

Feeling yourself awaken after the
hibernation of winter

The patchwork of different shades
of green in countryside fields

The purity of baby animals

Transitioning from hot foods to cold
foods, like a salad on the patio in a
hoodie instead of soup on the sofa with
a blanket

Warm evenings that remind you
summer is coming, only the bugs
haven't yet woken up

The collective happiness on
display at outdoor cafés and rooftop
happy hours

Not having to lug around a scarf, a hat,
gloves, and an oversize jacket (phew)

After-dinner walks as the days
get longer

Walking down the street on a sunny day
and having people smile at you

Seeing which resilient little blooms
survived the winter and are making
their return

The return of the birds!

The daintiness of eggs in a nest.

The honor and excitement you feel
peeking inside a nest.

Watching something grow

Falling back in love with taking walks

The crisscross lines of newly
mown grass

A quiet sunrise

Feeling the excitement of
summer's approach

Feeling alive again as you make plans
to celebrate in the sun

The beginning of the eating-what-you-
grow season

Sweet little deer and fawns, almost
invisible in the dusk light.

Visiting a botanical garden and
snapping photos of your
favorite plants

A mom and dad robin pair taking turns feeding the little ones in their nest.

The end of winter and the start of wanting to do things again!

Seeing a ladybug and counting the spots to know how old it is

Dappled sunshine

Increased outdoor time

Evenings you don't want to end, so you pretend it isn't just a bit chilly!

Enjoying the warmth when it comes and the cold when it revisits

The end-of-school-year excitement—the restless feeling both students and teachers experience.

Worms on wet pavement after a rainstorm.

Warmth without the humidity

Graduations!

Shimmering drops of morning dew

Tree frogs warming up their vocal cords.

A pink sunset as the sun's warmth fades

Watching ants shuffle in and out of their
ant hill

Looking at next week's forecast and not
seeing temperatures below freezing

Going on a walk and discovering
somewhere that feels like a
hidden oasis

The motion of water running
after melting.

When the evenings are loud as more insects wake up

The excitement of signing up for summer camp

Finally feeling like the big kid in school and knowing your way around (I think it's the same for regular life, too.)

When your sweet treats are in the fridge and the freezer

Fresh fruit that's in season.

The start of the spring farmers' market

Seeing what lies underneath months
of thick snow

Not needing snow boots every day

Kind of enjoying a cold day because it's
a friendly reminder of what you'll
soon miss

Knowing that even though wasps exist,
bumblebees do too

The end-of-school-year wrap-up days
(field day, celebrations, and so on)

Field trips!

Solar-powered patio lights

Popping in somewhere just to have a
drink because it's nice to be out and
about again

Gardening as an excuse to get outside
and ground yourself

Sidewalk chalk

Pastel floral wreaths on front doors

Marveling at how late it is yet how bright
it is outside

Outdoor suppers that feature herbs right from the garden.

✳

Getting a stray "Bless you" when you sneeze from allergies in public.

✳

Waiting for the bus on a beautiful day

✳

Taking a walk in the middle of the day and not needing a heavy jacket

✳

Going to the garden store and picking out new plants

✳

Leaving the windows open to air out the house while you spring clean

Having an outdoor space to relax in

Biking with the streets full of kids
enjoying the autonomy two
wheels provides

An open bench in the park.

Little kids playing on a playground.

Outdoor playdates—for kids and adults

Meeting the neighbors who moved in
during the winter

Flying a kite

Watching a baby snooze in
the sunshine

Timid little deer learning how to stay
alert in the backyard.

Okay, I have something nice to say
about pollen: the way it falls looks like
soft paint to be danced through.

New moms venturing out to show their
winter babies the world.

Outdoor music

Soft moss perfect for a fairy dance floor

Taking your hat off, running your fingers over your scalp, and feeling the cool air through your hair

The satisfying first few gulps of water after a workout

Putting on lip balm when your lips are chapped

A painted sunset with neon clouds

The familiarity of being yourself again after a long winter sleep.

Adults playing pickup ultimate frisbee.

The excitement in the air on the season's
first warm-enough-for-no-jacket day

How many different shades of green
exist in a single tree

Remembering you have a friend with a
lake house you're visiting this summer

No longer going home after work to
hibernate in bed

The miraculous magic of air-
conditioning that can only be
discovered on the first day you need it.

Making popsicles out of fruit juice

A rolling hill line slowly coming
into view.

Driving the same route home from
work every day and noticing the view
is a little greener each night

Meeting a friend and going for a
walk together

Remembering that bright yellow
dandelions are actually hardy
little weeds

The inevitable nature of how boys aged eight to eighteen, wear only shorts once the first sunny day of spring appears.

Little ones staying up past their bedtime after an end-of-year school performance.

Arching branches on either side of the sidewalk.

A little kid digging in a gravel driveway, sure they'll find a diamond.

Watching two raindrops race down a window and seeing which will win

Coffee in the morning outside in
the sun

Dogs snuggling up against you when you
wake up in the morning.

The smell after sleeping with the
windows cracked open

The warm wind that feels like kisses
instead of a cold, harsh stinging.

Hedging bets when going for a walk with
ominous clouds in the distance and
somehow winning against the rain

Baskets of just-planted flowers hung on
the porch, swaying in the wind.

The heroic nature of moving a worm
from the pavement after it rains.

Discovering a secret community garden

The quiet excitement of watching your
plants bloom.

Remembering that you're wearing
waterproof shoes and stomping
in puddles

Rain jackets on dogs

Warm pavement on a spring afternoon

Groups of kids walking home from
school, catching each other up on the
classroom excitements of the day.

Getting that funny feeling in your
stomach as you ride your bike over
hilly pavement

Nature finding a way to grow because
it's what it's meant to do—through
pavement, cracks, and fencing slats.

Finding a stick and pretending it's a
magic wand

Racing your siblings home from school

Someone teaching you how to eat honeysuckle from the vine.

The back-and-forth sound of a pickleball or tennis game in the morning air.

Finding a hidden bush of ripe blackberries

Taking your helmet off after a bike ride

A recommendation of a good book

Watching a baby discover the delight
of splashing in puddles

When setting goals to spend time
outside seems feasible again

Lying in the grass and imagining
yourself as the size of an ant in this
great big world

Finding shapes in clouds

Spotting squashed down trails
in grass marking a cyclist's
shortcut

Ivy growing up the side of a tree,
wrapping and winding its way around.

After-school snacks

The universally uncomfortable
experience of school bleachers

Eating dinner outside

Making mazes for ants with
sidewalk chalk

Being able to drive with the windows
down again

Going on a swing and remembering
how it feels to fly

Gathering flowers in a basket

Making daisy chains and necklaces

Watching a big kid helping a little kid

Evening sports practices

Pushing a little one in a swing

Purposely choosing a slower way home
so you can listen to a favorite song

Neighbors who bring trash cans in for each other.

Eating your lunch outside

The satisfaction of cleaning something— spending time and care on polishing and scrubbing.

Handprints in cement

Plants randomly growing next to one another.

The tenacious nature of weeds

Brick walls around a garden

The sunlight filtering through blades
of grass.

Evenings when it's still cool enough that
you only need the windows open
to sleep.

The lightness that spring cleaning a
closet can bring.

The squawking of a mama bird letting
you know you've come too close to
her nest.

Watching babies play (humans, animals;
it's all adorable)

Weeds growing through a crack in
the sidewalk.

Finding a table at a café with one chair
in the sun for you and one chair in the
shade for your friend

Motioning a pedestrian to cross
the street

Superhero moms pushing a stroller and
walking a dog at the same time.

A rabbit freezing in place and you
playing your part in its game by
pretending not to see them.

The satisfaction of turning on your
windshield wipers to clean
your windshield

The comfort of a familiar walking path

The time of year when ponds reappear
and disappear with the rain
and sunshine

Gorgeous groups of goslings

A "geese crossing" sign, showing that we all decided to prioritize these cute, fluffy goslings each season.

A row of geese with the babies with a mother and father as leader and caboose.

Teeny-tiny baby frogs along a creek bed.

How many times a flower can be reborn in one season

Discovering that some weeds are pretty

Noticing a broken branch in a tree, held aloft by its fellow branches

The excitement of returning to school for an evening end-of-year orchestra performance and being in the building after-hours.

The thrill of finding the perfect walking stick

Watching a pup realize their friend is walking toward them

The little white weeds that look like a tiny shower loofah.

Being near water, even if it isn't warm
enough yet to get in

Packing enough snacks for your hike

Finding your favorite pair of jelly sandals
from when you were five years old in
your adult size today

Moving somewhere new and seeing
what kind of plants come up during
your first spring there

Someone offering a drink of water at
the same moment you feel thirsty.

The first iced coffee of the season.

The synchronicity of baby birds in a nest popping their beaks up as mama bird lands with food.

How many shades of blue there are in a blue sky

Moving light jackets to the front of your closet and winter coats to the back

The aliveness of an evening with daylight past 8 p.m.

A bench with a worn-down spot
marking somebody's favorite seat.

The first barbecue of the season.

A fully defined rainbow (or even better,
a double rainbow!)

Watermelon or pineapple cubes
in a salad.

Seeing familiar squirrel friends for the
first time in months

Kindergartners' handmade Mother's
Day cards

Fluffy pink cherry blossoms blooming.

A sea of multicolored umbrellas seen
from a high vantage point.

The joyful chaotic scramble of an Easter
egg hunt

Frozen waterfalls waking up again, from
an icy drizzle to a downpour.

Looking up the name of a beautiful
flower you pass on a walk

Jumping over puddles on your morning
run, feeling like a kid

summer

An unplanned, synchronous chorus of
"Cows!" as everyone in the car spots
a herd.

The hot red cheeks of toddlers running
on a playground.

A cup of homemade lemonade from
a kid's roadside stand.

The feeling of warm sunshine on
your skin

Opening the windows throughout your
home to create a cross breeze

The waves getting darker as the sun sets.

The collective sigh of "We needed this"
as the clouds break open on a
humid afternoon.

The sounds of excitement and cheers
of evening Little League games

Watching a dog's eyes slowly close
in the evening sunshine

Sitting on a boardwalk edge
and dipping your feet in the cold water

Being a kid and realizing how popsicles are made (from this moment on, no juice is safe)

Morning cartoons on summer vacation

Waking up and walking outside without changing from your pj's to enjoy your cup of coffee on the patio

The satisfaction of building something with Lego

The countdown to a summer vacation

Waking up early to get in the car for
a road trip

✳

Not being cold when you walk out the
door in the morning

✳

Cherishing an afternoon thunderstorm

✳

Holding your breath underwater
in the pool

✳

How early the birds start to sing on
a midsummer morning

✳

The comforting sound of crickets
in the evening

Having air-conditioning in your car

The tickle of a bead of sweat threatening
to roll down your forehead.

Going camping alone or with friends

Staying up late to the sound of tree frogs

Summer camp

The way little-kid sweat smells different
from adult sweat.

The joy of not needing to get out of bed
right when you wake up.

Workplace lunches taking a little longer
on an outdoor patio

The surprising relief a paper
fan can offer.

Wandering without a timeline or task

Getting a Slurpee on a hot
summer afternoon

✹

The rhyming songs kids sing while
skipping rope.

✹

The relief of someone else
remembering the bug spray.

Remembering to wear the little shorts that prevent chafing

Evening barbecues

The idea that someone is having their best summer ever right now.

The quick camaraderie that comes from sleepaway camp.

When little kids draw the sun wearing sunglasses.

Taking your feet off the pedals of your bike as you roar down the hill

The universal agony of scraping your
toe in the pool.

The relief when you break the pool's
surface after being underwater just
a little too long.

The smell of sunscreen

An evening spent outdoors

The glistening ocean sparkling like gems
on the wave tips.

The way you can smell the sea before
you can see it while driving to the beach.

The relief of walking into an air-conditioned establishment on a too-hot day.

✳

The luxury of walking out of too-cold air-conditioning into a hot day.

✳

Baseball games

✳

Sundresses and summer linens

✳

Rocking chairs on porches.

✳

Enjoying an early sunrise on a drive to work

Drying off by lying down on the side
of the pool

Realizing that comfortable clothes were
the right call for an amusement park
in July

The ridiculous speed at which ice
cream melts.

Waving to a neighbor as you walk
by their porch

Falling asleep in the sunshine

Long, late-summer evening shadows

How summer vacation friends always
feel like best friends

Being asked to help with a clue for
a summer camp scavenger hunt

Making a fairy house in the garden only
out of items found around you in nature

Daffodil heads always moving toward
the sun.

Coming home to family having a glass
of wine on their back porch, with one
waiting for you in the kitchen

A dog smiling in the sunshine.

The gentle pace of a ladybug

A nap after a day in the sun.

Going down waterslides as a kid

Going down waterslides as an adult

The unspoken agreement that
swimming counts as bathing at least one
night a week during the summer.

Sunglasses on dogs.

The cool spray of bug spray.

Using a new bottle of sunscreen without
the fear of it running out

The lazy rumble of a thunderstorm in
the distance that never appears.

Walking through the neighborhood and
counting how many neighbors had the
same idea of grilling on a hot
summer eve

Seeing lazy gnats float in the
dappled sunlight

The enormous strength of a tree to withstand a powerful summer storm.

Birds circling the skies ahead.

Someone somewhere is having their first taste of ice cream.

Your reflection in a creek.

Walking up to a deer, cautiously and quietly

The simplicity of making tie-dyed T-shirts.

Making an ice cream sundae

Heat rising off the pavement.

Water sparkling in the sunshine.

Going to the farm to pick fresh fruit

Birds getting quiet as they observe
a midday siesta when the day
gets too hot.

Standing in a cross breeze

Walking to a coffee shop

The simple joy of an
ice cream sandwich.

✹

Someone teaching you how to do
a handstand underwater.

✹

Racing a speed radar on foot to see
how fast you are

✹

A big, thick, luxurious towel to wrap up
in after bathing.

✹

The smell of hot asphalt.

✹

A mama bird returning to use the same
nest again for the summer season.

The high-pitched squeal all kids make
when jumping in the pool.

✳

The power of a splash.

✳

Feeling sand shift underneath your toes

✳

Campfires

✳

Bonfires

✳

Someone teaching you how to
make s'mores.

✳

Rediscovering old favorite playlists

Underestimating the heat and feeling
relieved when home comes into view at
the end of a walk

A squirrel's pounce.

Someone bringing an iced coffee for
you at work because they stopped
for themselves and thought of you.

The satisfaction of building
a sandcastle.

When you have to be outside on a
summer morning and you wear
a hoodie because it's cold.

The speed of a summer thunderstorm.

The bright colors of flowers in
flowerbeds.

Butterflies flitting by, impossible to catch.

Sitting on the porch in the evening

The pavement staying warm long after
the sun's gone down.

The joyful simplicity of kicking a ball
with someone.

The way a storm can clear out
the humidity.

✳

Floating on water

✳

The sun's warmth soaking into your skin.

✳

Ice in your drink on a summer's day.

✳

A pair of cardinals resting on a fence.

✳

A green spot in the middle of a forest,
ripe with magic.

✳

Watching the clouds move

Reaching for a water bottle that's kept
your water cold all day

Catching a cricket

Staying up late and discovering the
excitement a summer night brings

Having the perfect summer wardrobe
of clothes that keep you cool,
comfortable, and confident

Going across the monkey bars

Using a school's playground when
school is out for the summer

Cheeks and fingers sticky from ice pops

Catching a puddle on the sidewalk
before it evaporates in the heat

The increased frequency of seeing
an empty email inbox.

The soft flapping of bats emerging
at dusk.

Watching a bird swoop low with a keen
sense of where it is spatially

Someone holding your hands while you
learn to roller-skate.

Bright sunlight bouncing off the corner of your bedroom as an early summer morning greeting.

Going on holiday, near or far; remembering it doesn't take much distance to feel like you've gone far

Sitting in the passenger seat with your eyes closed, wind blowing through your hair

The mist rising from the pavement after a summer storm.

Lightning bugs

A tiny glimpse of starlight, here and there, as fireflies glitter around you.

Staying up past bedtime with no plans for tomorrow

Putting yourself to bed before bedtime

The deep rest that comes upon awakening from a nap after a day of sunshine and water.

Blasting your favorite song in the car with the windows down on a summer eve

The busyness of nature—plants, animals, insects, the weather

Sitting underneath a tree in the park and people watching

Tire swings

The sound of sprinklers going off in the early morning and evening.

A dark cloud skyline across a bright-blue sky.

How the rain falls straight down when there is no wind

Raindrops dripping off an overhead
branch after a storm has ended.

✳

Jumping into water

✳

Lying in the shallow section of a pool
with a clear blue sky above

✳

Wet leaves being hit by the sunset
and glittering like sparkles.

✳

Cute fairy lights around the porch
while you enjoy a meal with the
people you love.

✳

Bringing a guitar to a campsite

The lazy slap of a dog's tail on a front porch as you walk up.

Being outside in the rain because it isn't cold and it feels good

Playing cornhole

Getting together with family and friends on a weeknight

Seeing a movie in an air-conditioned theater on a hot day with a big slushy

Catch-ups on the patio with a good friend.

The relief of putting on a pair of sunglasses.

✳

Finding sunglasses that feel comfortable on your head

✳

Finding sunglasses that look good on you

✳

Walking through a creek

✳

Pulling long hair into a ponytail and feeling the relief of a breeze on the back of your neck

✳

Strawberry-picking season

Taking a shower and falling asleep on clean sheets under a fan

The consistent pinging of an overhead fan that's gone slightly off-balance.

A fat dog in a kiddie pool.

Remembering that you can go and buy fancy ice cream that you never got to have growing up

The closeness that comes from traveling with a friend.

Going on vacation by yourself

Babies in swimsuits.

Babies in floaties.

Grown-ups in floaties.

Crickets and frogs bellowing through
the night.

The way the flow of water is never the
same twice.

How it feels so much easier to eat
vegetables when they're all in season

Drive-in movies

Raindrops down a window reflected
in your outfit, patterning you with
polka dots.

Finding a summer song

Showering sand off your body

Cold iced tea with a wedge of lemon

Grabbing whatever produce is in the
fridge and making a "salad"

Raindrops in different shapes and sizes
from the same cloud.

The sound of rain from inside
a parked car.

Finding a covered spot as a spontaneous
storm hits

Feeling the sun soak into your skin

Taking a flight and remembering the sky
is always blue; sometimes there's just
stuff in the way

When your windshield wipers match up
with the wipers on the car in front
of yours.

Fuzzy caterpillars munching on leaves.

Lightning flashing across the sky.

Learning to count between
thunderclaps and lightning strikes to
determine a storm's distance away

Mist rising from the road that feels like
driving through clouds.

Horses at pasture.

Dogs who love to swim when presented
with the opportunity.

Finding an open table by the window
at a café

Watching a little one gather the bravery
to jump off the diving board

Catching fireflies as a kid

Corn on the cob

Someone teaching you how to skip
a stone over a lake.

Little siblings holding hands in
double strollers.

A spontaneous game of amateur
beach volleyball.

The careful craft of packing the perfect picnic basket.

Blowing bubbles for babies to chase around and pop

Finding a painted rock at the park

Squealing kids running through jets and sprinklers on a splash pad

Live music spilling out of restaurants onto the street.

Outdoor concerts with food trucks in the parking lot.

Red heart-shaped sunglasses

Dads carrying their toddlers on their
shoulders at crowded events.

Mosquito-repellant candles for
backyard meals

The fizzy white foam on the crest
of a wave

The music of an approaching
ice cream truck.

Ringing your bell as you bike past
a jogger

How connected to nature you feel while swimming in natural bodies of water—lakes, oceans, rivers, even sinkholes!

Open-toed sandals to let your hot feet breathe.

The periwinkle blue of a completely cloudless sky.

Moms doing yoga in a park.

Moms doing yoga on the beach.

The first lick of a soft-serve ice cream cone on a sweltering day.

The little crates that farmers market
berries come in.

✳

Silly children's bike helmets—with
mohawks, horns, or crazy colors.

✳

The colorful tassels on the handlebars
of a child's bike.

✳

The pride that comes with removing
your training wheels as a kid.

✳

A refreshing fruit salad!

✳

Lying down to watch the stars and
seeing more and more appear

Little kids in sports equipment.

Swimming in the summer rain
on purpose

Seeing a wedding party in a
public place

A streak of sunscreen a child
accidentally left on their cheek.

Reading on a balcony at sunset

Spritzing water on your face with
a spray bottle on a hot, dry day

The momentary midair thrill as you
jump into a cold pool.

✳

Yelling "cannonball" before making
a huge splash

✳

How the texture of your hair changes
by the beach

✳

Screaming with a friend at the drop
of a rickety rollercoaster

✳

The people who are content to wait
and watch while their friends ride
a rickety rollercoaster.

Fall

Finding money in the pocket of a jacket
you haven't worn since last year

The sound of rain pitter-pattering on the
roof as you wake.

The satisfying crunch of driving over
fallen leaves.

The satisfaction of walking on
crunchy leaves.

Flannel on dogs

Flannel everything

The wind whipping up fallen leaves into little cyclones across the pavement.

Waking up to frost coating the ground, like a little preview of snow

Realizing you can enjoy sitting outside without the summer heat making it uncomfortable

Noticing how a change in season is often first visible in the mornings

Walking outside and not immediately sweating

The excitement of returning to school
to see your friends again.

The smell of a freshly sharpened pencil.

How much easier it is to schedule
get-togethers with friends now that
everyone is done traveling for
the season.

Crisp, red apples straight from the tree.

Families in which one kid carves a
spooky but cute pumpkin face, and the
other one carves a scary face.

The excitement of picking out your Halloween costume.

Switching from iced coffee to hot coffee

The collective human excitement of wearing clothes in season.

The reintroduction of jackets

Hiking on a fall day and the movement keeping you warm

The yellows and golds and oranges of sunshine and the changing leaves.

Fallen leaves on the ground, like an autumn carpet.

Shuffling your feet through dried leaves on the path, kicking them up as you go

The reveal of a view beyond the trees as they shed their leaves on your local walking path.

The stubborn green still holding on when everything else has changed.

The way a squirrel will hide its loot in a nest only to forget where it is season after season.

Squirrels busying themselves by stuffing their cheeks with acorns.

How you can tell which direction gets more sunlight through the day, depending on the speed with which the leaves turn colors.

Making fairy drinking cups from acorn shells

Going for a drive down an autumn-colored lane

🍁

The renewed energy that comes after a more laid-back summer season.

Starting again

Leveling up—a new grade, new
classroom, new season, new quarter

The joy when summer temperatures
return for one final day well into the
fall season, like a sweet farewell
to the memories and a swift kick
to the humidity.

The first morning you go outside
and can see your breath.

Pulling out your favorite thick
cardigan to wrap up in

Lighting a candle on a cozy fall evening

The sudden drop to freezing
temperatures one night before they
bounce back to the milder
autumnal temperatures.

Finding a perfect fallen leaf, no rips or
tears, just a dazzling terra-cotta shade

Cooler evenings spent watching
outdoor sporting games and practices.

When you realize your drink upon
coming home has turned from a glass
of iced tea to a mug of hot tea.

The reminder that retreating, slowing down, and even death can be part of growing back stronger.

The smell of a bonfire

The sound of twigs snapping and fire crackling as you gather for a s'mores-making session.

The absolute impossibility of walking silently through a woodland trail in autumn.

Warm spiced candles

The resistance boys have to wearing a jacket.

❋

Pumpkin candles, pumpkin coffee, pumpkin bread

❋

The collective gasp from a road trip crew taking in a fall panorama.

❋

The thrill that comes when parking in the grass for a festival.

❋

Walking through a farmers' market and the smell of autumn goods surrounding you

Finding the perfect reading nook in your favorite bookshop or library

A night in bingeing a show with a scented candle burning on your coffee table.

'Tis the season of layers!

The dusty smell of hay.

The crisp smell of fall air

Watching a scary movie with a friend who screams and jumps at everything

A thick blanket and a book with a world
to get lost in.

Pressing a perfect red leaf in between
the pages of a book

The collective energy we, as a human
species, have put into making everything
pumpkin spice.

Revisiting an old teacher when you're
in a higher grade

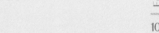

A student visiting you and looking so
much older in just a few months.

Chunky and thick oversized sweaters

The slick slipperiness of leaves on the
ground after a storm.

The smell of fallen wet leaves

The first fire in a fireplace in a
new home.

The sound of a fireplace in the
background while you watch a show
on the couch in the living room.

The dread and excitement of school
charity runs.

How falling leaves allow us a chance
to see them, to take in their shapes,
differences, and colors—what used
to be out of sight now in reach.

The speed with which spring farm
babies have grown to near adults
by autumn.

Apple cider—served cold after an
afternoon in the sun, then served
hot around a firepit as the evening
cools off.

How entrancing the flickering of
candlelight is

When it's cool enough to eat
lunch outside.

Rain boots for babies

Kids wearing matching raincoats.

Baking—the process, the patience,
the payoff

An insect friend landing on the tip of
your finger, catching its breath before
flying on.

The ability to cuddle up in a jacket
during the evenings

Evening football games

The appearance of pumpkins
everywhere

Someone somewhere is carving their
first pumpkin.

How many types of gourds there are.

The way light flickers from inside
a carved pumpkin.

How, during Halloween, every creak
and slam makes you jump.

The delight of believing in ghost stories.

Someone teaching you to hold a
flashlight under your chin to create that
spooky face.

The introduction of cooked meals back
into the daily menu

Spaghetti squash

Adding a cozy quilt to your lighter
bed linens

The anticipation of the
upcoming holidays

When you realize it must be fall because you can see your neighbor's house through the thinning trees.

The therapeutic nature of an audiobook on a rainy day.

The slow swooping of a lonely leaf falling from a higher branch.

A fresh journal, a new notebook, school supplies for adults

How many shades of orange there are

The saying "trick or treat!"

The way hay feels, scratchy and poking in some ways but also smooth and silky in others.

Sitting on a hay bale

The way it feels to run your fingers through dried corn at one of those fall farm festivals.

Apple and cinnamon blending to create the ultimate autumnal combination.

So many flannel shirts and patterns at a farm festival.

The show-off nature of pine trees as all
the other trees begin to shed their leaves.

The reassuring consistency of seasons—
birth, bloom, reclaim, hibernation.

A tree full of yellow leaves

Hats that cover your ears.

Jumping into a pile of leaves

Watching an excited furry friend throw
themselves into a neatly collected pile
of leaves

The perplexing shapes of gourds

Running your finger over the smooth
edges of a color-changing leaf

A thermos of hot chocolate and a
flannel picnic blanket for the perfect
foliage picnic

The urge to nest and make our homes
cozier as the temperatures drop and we
know we'll be spending more time
at home.

Putting up fall decorations on the first
day of September

The way raindrops through a window
distort headlights and streetlamps.

Dodging raindrops as you walk to the
coffee shop to commiserate with
someone over a hot drink

The full moon on a crisp evening

Being grateful for heating systems as you
step indoors

Wearing plush pajamas to bed

The days getting dark earlier and
cooler faster.

Cool morning fog on a mirrorlike
still lake

Going for a hike and feeling like
you're on a mission to discover
something profound

The multipurpose nature of scarves

Realizing pulling a hat over your ears
works kind of the same as noise-
canceling headphones

The combined sound of leaves and
twinkling wind chimes.

The gentler nature of the sun—less
overwhelming and more welcomed

Warm woolen socks

The collective cheer from viewers
as the final runner finishes the race.

Pouring creamer into hot coffee and
watching the ripples gently move to the
outward edge of the cup

Putting your finger into a stream and
watching the cold water separate
and then rejoin again

Frosty mornings when you immediately throw on a robe and a pair of socks.

Pine cones!

The vital, versatile vest.

Keeping an extra sweatshirt in the car for when you're out and cold

Friday evening sports night at the local park

The reds of the leaves varying from the softest cherry tint to the deepest burgundy.

Watching a furry friend take in the wind,
closing their eyes and sniffing the air

Feeling gratitude for cooler
temperatures when a hot day rolls in
one random October morning

The perfect temperature for furry
friends to be outside and not get too hot
or cold.

The glorious excitement of book fairs

*

Trimming the last of the blooms
to bring inside for a reminder
of summer

Pressing flowers

✻

A duck sleeping while standing up, its
neck wound back and snuggled into
its feathers.

✻

Geese swimming in a row.

✻

Passing a lake on a favorite walk and
noticing the goslings are looking more
and more like the adults

✻

Grandpa sweaters

✻

A bouquet of red, yellow, gold, and
orange flowers from the farmers' market.

Throwing handfuls of leaves into
the air like confetti

Driving home and thinking how cozy
all the houses look through the rain

The comfort of sitting around a firepit
with someone you love.

A cat falling asleep on the pavement.

A dog sleeping next to the campfire.

Driving through a tunnel of dappled
red leaves

The dainty way cinnamon puffs into the
air as you measure it for muffins.

✳

Kicking pine cones on a walk

✳

The magic of realizing a whole oak tree
lives inside an acorn.

✳

Coming across an old building on a hike
and imagining its history

✳

How the leaves wave in the wind,
holding on strong to their branches.

✳

A coffee lid that's never on quite right.

Babies in backpacks on hikes.

Adults wishing they were a baby in a
backpack halfway through a hike.

Catching a Halloween movie marathon
on TV

The fun of scaring yourself with a
horror movie.

Regretting watching a scary movie
at bedtime

The short period of time where the
temperature is ideal for fingerless gloves.

The reflection of a fall sunset in
a window

Hot chocolate with grated orange peel

Crafty markets, perfect for
holiday shopping

The leftovers of a roast dinner

Picking out your favorite candy to give to
trick-or-treaters

Eating a lot of the candy you bought for
trick-or-treaters

Seeing teachers dressed up for the class costume parade

Seeing leaves gathering along a glittery riverside

Cross-country season!

Neighbors who put up geese-crossing signs at the end of their driveways.

Looking back at some of the Halloween costumes you chose as a kid and being grateful your parents not only embraced but also encouraged your weirdness

Guessing which of the leaves will turn first on the trees on your drive home and seeing if you're right just a few weeks later

The speed leaves change once the process begins.

The simplicity of a baked apple with a sprinkle of cinnamon and brown sugar.

When someone remembers to go out ahead of you to warm your car up.

When you remember to warm your car up!

The reintroduction of a routine
after summer

The ones who get a little too excited
about switching up their wardrobe and
wind up in boots and a scarf on a hot
autumn day.

The ones who are a little too confident
and wind up in basketball shorts at the
bus stop on a brisk day.

The day you realize that the trees are
almost bare and winter is almost here.

The sweetness of little, tiny pumpkins.

The incredible (and sustainable) invention of potpourri.

✱

Thinking ahead and bringing a cardigan

✱

The sweetness of the almost-too-ripe fruit at the end of a season

✱

Evenings on the porch with a warm drink, blanket, or both

✱

Roasting marshmallows over a campfire

✱

Houses that go all-out with Halloween decorations.

Feeling grateful for the dual-purpose
nature of over-the-ear headphones as
temperatures drop in the evening

Chunky socks and thick-knit cardigans

Walking through a pumpkin patch with
everyone around you determined to
find the perfect one

The way sparks of a campfire float into
the velvet darkness of an evening.

A brilliantly sunny day with a cool,
crisp breeze

Winter

The sun shining off the snow, sparkling like glitter.

❆

Driving through the snow, pretending you're in a spaceship, zooming through space

❆

The crunch of stepping through snow the morning after a significant snowfall.

❆

Stepping into a warm house after being out in the cold

❆

The rosy-red cheeks of bundled-up children.

Sitting by a fireplace, reading a book,
and listening to the crackling wood

❄

Breathing in the steam of a hot shower
and feeling your muscles slowly relax

❄

The pink of a sunrise dancing off the
morning frost.

❄

A thermos keeping your tea warm
on a cold winter's commute.

❄

Falling asleep in warm flannel sheets

❄

A terry cloth bathrobe to wrap up
in on a cold morning

Red cardinals as a pop of color against
a winter landscape.

❄

Kids squealing as they throw snowballs
at each other on the way to the
school bus.

❄

Warm, fuzzy socks for shuffling around
the house

❄

The smell of a fire in a fireplace

❄

Wood-wicked candles that make the
sound of a fire crackling while lit.

❄

A thermos of soup!

A clear, crisp, starry night

❄

Your breath making little puffs of smoke
on a winter's walk.

❄

Decorating for the holidays

❄

Going to see a winter parade with
a warm drink in hand

❄

Suggesting your favorite obscure cheesy
holiday movie, and expecting no one
else to have seen it, only for someone
to say, "I love that movie."

Hats on dogs

The way it smells just before it starts
to snow—cold and fresh.

❄

The specific shade of white the sky
turns before it begins to snow.

❄

Nourishing, satisfying, and filling meals

❄

Hot, homemade soup

❄

Tearing into a hot baguette, sacrificing
your fingertips for that first bite

❄

Finding the most perfect mug for hot
cocoa, with extra space for
marshmallows

The ritual of making a mug of tea.

✳

The season of seeing family you might
not get to see regularly.

✳

Feeling grateful that you don't regularly
have to see the family you see during
the season

✳

The way we stomp our feet
and blow on our hands to stay
warm outside.

✳

Emergency hand warmers tucked into
the ends of mittens or the bottoms
of pockets.

Someone teaching you about
Santa Claus.

❄

The magic of Christmas lights twinkling
on porches and around rooftops.

❄

Celebrating the holiday season with
town traditions

❄

Being bundled up and warm
on a freezing day

❄

When you remember to wear
two pairs of socks.

❄

Kids in brightly colored snowpants

The sanctity of traditions

❄

Meals cooked with the intent of sharing.

❄

Adults embracing the magic
of the holidays.

❄

Growing up and realizing just how
much work adults must do to make
holidays magical

❄

How the irresistible smoothness of a
holly leaf merits the risk of pricking your
finger on the pointy ends.

Kid-sized snow shovels

The pretty contrast of red berries to the green holly backdrop.

✻

Fresh footprints in the snow

✻

An unseasonably warm day that prompts everyone to get outside and soak up the sunshine while it lasts.

✻

The sunrise over the frosty lawn, where sunbeams bounce off like the glitter of a disco ball.

✻

Stepping into a warm café after being outside on a cold day

The never-ending balancing act of
putting layers on and removing them as
you shift from indoors to outdoors.

❄

The luxury of a pearl-shaded coat
designed for evenings out on the town.

❄

Keeping a thick, fluffy blanket on the
end of every sofa

❄

A furry friend bounding across
the snow.

❄

The flash of orange as a fox runs across
a snowy field.

The confusing allure of eggnog

A baby so bundled up that you can barely see their eyes.

Watching a toddler try to stand in the snow

Strolling around a bookstore on a cold, rainy night, followed by dinner and reading in bed

The warmth from a sip of a hot drink flowing through you and warming you up from the inside out.

The satisfying puffs of hot air that come from a sunny outdoor walk with a fast pup.

Putting your coat on and remembering how much you loved it when you first bought it

Candlelit dinners

Sending a card to someone saying you miss them

Finding the best holiday cards for the season

Two red cardinals sweeping over
a frosty lawn.

✻

The relief of sinking into your
car seat after an evening in
uncomfortable shoes.

✻

Tracing shapes on the windows
of a frosty car

✻

A neighbor helping shovel snow.

✻

A neighbor with a snowblower.

✻

The silence of a snowy day in
the woods

Someone else scraping your
windshield for you.

❄

Seat warmers in your car

❄

The undeniable anticipation of
having meals and treats that come
only once a year.

❄

The excitement of a countdown.

❄

The strange limbo of the week between
Christmas and New Year's

❄

How each individual snowflake
is unique.

Evenings cuddled up watching
an old favorite show or movie.

✻

The smell of gingerbread

✻

A velvet night sky speckled with stars.

✻

Leaving footprints in the snow

✻

Someone teaching you how to make
a snow angel.

✻

Bundling up to go for a walk

✻

Winter hikes

The silence of footsteps through powdery snow

❄

The traditions and stories behind handed-down recipes.

❄

Dunking hot bread into stew to soak up the last bits

❄

Settling in by the fireplace

❄

Getting snowed in

❄

Jumping into a soft snow pile from a good height

The hibernation of nature—the grass, the plants, the leaves.

❄

Animals tucking themselves away for a long winter's sleep.

❄

Giving a gift you're excited for the recipient to open

❄

Hunkering down through a storm

❄

Picking out a treat to hunker down with

❄

The neighbor who leaves their holiday lights up the longest.

The neighbor who takes their holiday
lights down right away.

❄

Milky sunlight barely breaking through
the clouds.

❄

Being tucked into bed, under a thick
layer of blankets, and sinking into
soft pillows

❄

Warming your fingertips on a mug
of hot tea

❄

Taking a leisurely hot bath at night
because you don't have to get up early

Peppermint sticks

❄

The excitement of a winter recital.

❄

The haunting sound of a winter's gale.

❄

A pair of swans on an icy lake

❄

The thrill of mastering ice skating.

❄

Branches hanging low, weighed
down with ice.

❄

Icicles forming along the
roof's edge.

The luck of finding a perfectly formed
icicle within arm's reach.

✻

Low-strung lights between shops
on either side of the street

✻

The sizzle of sleet hitting the rooftop.

✻

Meeting a furry friend on a walk who
was made for the outdoors and is in
their element!

✻

The satisfying shake a muddy pup does
as soon as their paws step back indoors.

✻

The peculiar shape of pine cones

The collective excitement before a
big snow

❄

The way the late-evening sun outlines
the edges of snowflakes frozen to
the window.

❄

Babies going sledding for the first time.

❄

Grown-ups overjoyed to share sledding
with a new human for the first time.

❄

Sticking out your tongue as snow falls

❄

The way holiday lights illuminate the
street outside your window.

The satisfying nature of thick,
fat snowflakes

❋

Rewatching the holiday episodes of
your favorite shows

❋

A leaf wholly encased in a thin layer
of ice.

❋

Driving through fog on an early
morning, feeling like you're in a cloud

❋

The necessary foot stomp as you come
in from the muddy streets.

❋

The sound of a crackling fire.

Stews, casseroles, and soups—the season of warm, nourishing meals.

❄

Heading out for a walk and having the path to yourself

❄

Ice forming along the edges of a river bed, while chunks gather where the water is shallowest.

❄

Slicing oranges and simmering them on the stove in water, cloves, and cinnamon

❄

The welcoming feeling of warmth when the winter sun soaks into your black winter jacket.

No mosquitoes!

No pollen!

❄

Chopped firewood next to the fireplace
to last through the storm.

❄

How many types of cookies there are
to try in the world.

❄

Learning about the traditions of
someone you love

❄

Drying your clothes off after a day
of sledding

An inventive homemade sled

❄

Tucking your toes down into the bottom
of your bed

❄

The way snow looks falling in front
of a lit streetlamp.

❄

The excitement of holiday displays
in shops as a child.

❄

Finding the absolute perfect gift
for someone

❄

A store clerk smiling through the chaos
of holiday shopping.

Finding the perfect gift for yourself when you're shopping for someone else

❄

Waking up after a frost and seeing everything perfectly encapsulated in ice

❄

The childlike anticipation of going to sleep with snow falling, excited to wake up and see how deep it is.

❄

How a snowy backdrop makes a group of deer visible.

❄

Pom-poms on hats

❄

Pom-poms on hats on babies

Videos of dogs trying to walk with their snow shoes on.

❄

The gathering of twinkling lights of a town as you fly over in a plane.

❄

Sinking into a hot tub when it is freezing outside

❄

Someone reaching out their hand to steady you when walking on a slippery pavement.

❄

The surprising peace that comes from being in the mountains.

Staying in and having a game night

❄

Watching snow completely cover
another person while you're walking

❄

The charm of holiday twinkle lights

❄

Cheesy holiday movies

❄

Town gatherings and seasonal parades

❄

The entrepreneurship of teenage boys
shoveling driveways.

❄

A snowy mountain landscape

Someone somewhere is seeing snow
for the first time this season.

✳

When it turns out your snow boots
are waterproof.

✳

A churning gray ocean, frothy and frigid,
washing a beach with cold, wet sand.

✳

Someone giving you a
thoughtful present.

✳

Having at least double the amount of
candy than needed when decorating
a gingerbread house—for the
construction and architect's fee

Horses letting out a puff of warm breath
as they stomp their hooves on a
cold day.

✻

Eating lunch outside at a café because
they have heaters and firepits to keep
you warm

✻

A café with comfy lounge chairs
and fireplaces.

✻

A lake so still you have to throw a stone
to see whether it's frozen.

✻

Having a place to bundle up and enjoy
your morning coffee outside

Walking into a friend's house and it smells like a bakery

✻

Finding a singular brave little bud that decided to show up a bit too early

✻

Sweet robins on a gate in the lukewarm afternoon sun.

✻

How a furry friend can find the perfect patch of sunlight in the house.

✻

How good it feels to step outside into fresh air when you've been cooped up somewhere with the heating too high.

Being mesmerized while examining the snowflakes landing in your palm

❄

Having a tissue when you need it

❄

How good hot tea feels on a sore throat.

❄

Someone offering a cough drop when you've got a tickle in your throat.

❄

A day in winter when the whole household—even the dog—has a runny nose.

❄

That subconscious countdown of a new year, ripe with possibility.

That a snow day is a natural sign to take
a slow day

❄

Embracing the idea that humans are
perhaps not meant to become new
versions of themselves in the new year
but that it might be better to time it
with spring

❄

A season of rest and recovery, however
that looks for you.

❄

Learning from a bear that it's OK
to hibernate

❄

Finding the perfect pair of
house slippers

How slowly snow builds up compared
to how fast it melts when you're a child.

❄

How slowly snow melts compared to
how fast it builds up when you're
an adult.

❄

The majestic stillness of a forest
of pine trees

❄

Candles that smell like pine trees,
bringing the outdoors in with
the season.

❄

How the repetitive patterns of winter
weather are signs from the universe to
settle into rituals and healing.

A full moon on a snowy field, reflecting bright as sunlight.

The collective experience of it taking much longer to get ready to leave the house because of all the layers you're putting on.

Playing outside during school and complaining about being cold—every teacher's response being to run around to warm up

❄

Big, impressive, well-decorated snowmen next to small, wonky, haphazard snowmen.

Retail workers who show up to help
keep the world go round through the
holiday season.

❄

Radio stations that commit to playing
only holiday music throughout
the season.

❄

The sense of community that comes
from singing songs together in public.

❄

Realizing how hard it is to run through
deep snow

❄

Gingerbread men decorated with
different outfits and faces.

Programming your out-of-office automatic email response at work

✽

The joy of complimentary candy canes

✽

Removing your layers of clothes while shoveling snow because you're working up a sweat

✽

When the tips of your ears and nose get pleasantly numb in the cold.

✽

Strolling through a Christmas tree farm

✽

The question, "What's your favorite holiday song?"

Realizing the snow is "packing snow" and will make the perfect, round snowball soon

❄

When the night seems oddly light because the sky and ground are white.

❄

Snow piling up like little hats on car side mirrors.

❄

Waking up a child by opening the curtains to reveal the winter wonderland created overnight

❄

Thinking of the fish resting far below the icy surface of lakes

When a smooth layer of snow
coats every roof and chimney like
icing on a cake.

❄

Snow getting caught on eyelashes.

❄

Trying to hold onto a friend's sled before
hitting a bump and careening apart

❄

Twinkly lights winding up a tree trunk.

❄

Being the first to walk through an
untouched field of snow

❄

The extra-sweet layer of colorful icing
on an already-sweet sugar cookie.

Kids climbing on piled up snowbanks.

❄

Groups of friends ice skating, the good
skaters helping the bad.

❄

The concept of skiing—sliding down
a snowy mountain on strips of wood

❄

Making vanilla whipped cream from
scratch for your coffee or hot chocolate

❄

Using the extra holiday time to reread
a favorite childhood book series

❄

Seeing a kid reading your favorite
childhood book series for the first time

Cozy family board game nights that get too competitive.

❄

Family skate hours at the local ice rink.

❄

The last day of school before winter break when teachers plan a movie for class.

❄

Watching a figure skater spin on the tip of her skate

❄

People who like to snowshoe.

❄

Matching sets of hats and mittens

A rabbit leaping through the snow.

❄

Leaving cookies for Santa Claus and dad
sneakily eating them before bed

❄

Driving by a snowy hill and thinking,
"That's a good one for sledding."

❄

The thunder of little feet waking up the
house on Christmas morning.

❄

A dog's paw-prints in the snow.

❄

Baking holiday cookies to share
with friends

Everyday

Crossing something off your to-do list

Closing your laptop at the end of
a workday

Lighting a new candle and its scent filling
the room

Seeing a photo of yourself as a child
and feeling proud of the person
you've become

The slow, steady rise and fall of a pet's
belly when it's sleeping soundly.

The satisfied ache in your legs and feet
after a long day of walking.

Turning on your car to find a favorite
song just beginning

The first sip of a hot cup of coffee

The smell of fresh coffee filling your
home as you get ready in the morning.

The delight of finding a snack you forgot
you bought.

Waving to a neighbor walking down
the street

Whistling a tune and hitting all the
right notes

Petting a friendly dog who's excited
to meet you as you happen to
walk by

When you realize you handled a
situation better than you would have
in the past.

Watching a bird glide on the wind,
swooping and floating serenely

When someone lets you go ahead of
them in line at the grocery store.

The kindness of a stranger helping a
neighbor cross the street.

A fresh notebook full of blank pages,
ready for dreams and plans.

Someone walking by wearing a scent
that brings back happy memories.

The addition of a new furry friend
to the family

Waking up to a day that's entirely yours,
with nothing to do and nowhere to be

When the main character finally realizes
they're in love.

Naming your car or your bike

Sleeping in your own bed after
being away

Having a friend whose conversation
feels like a break in the clouds after
a storm

Listening to a song that speaks to exactly
what you need to hear

The gentle nudges of a furry friend
inviting you to pet them.

A recipe handed down
through generations.

Your computer locating the printer on
the first attempt—and there's ink!

Discovering an extra French fry at the
bottom of the bag

When you mention you're hungry
and someone offers you a snack.

The airport arrivals lounge after an
international flight lands.

Missing a friend and then randomly
seeing a text pop up: "Just wanted
to say hi!"

Being able to give someone assistance
when they're down

The sigh of relief when you make it to
your destination after driving on empty.

Making a pot of coffee when a friend
comes over, knowing you'll soon be
sipping and laughing together

Filling a glass perfectly full and it
doesn't spill over

Having a day off where nobody needs
anything from you

Finding the perfect lighting in the most unexpected place, such as a grocery store bathroom

A friend who listens, not judges.

How birdhouses look like little versions of human houses.

The relief that comes from starting a project you've been putting off because it felt intimidating.

Deep sofas with soft fabric, cozy blankets, and comfortable pillows

The way humans get excited collectively during an eclipse, the Olympics, or *The Great British Baking Show.*

Watching someone excel at their craft— woodworking, singing, coaching, or healing

Front porches (petition for all homes to have a front porch where we can gather with neighbors and decorate for the seasons)

Pulling into the driveway after a long drive

Rediscovering old favorite playlists

Getting into the car and your seat is already set in your position.

Your favorite coworker's quirks that make the day go a little faster.

Doing something good for someone just because you can

Having a space of your own—a home, room, car, bench

Waking up from a nap feeling rested and hazy

The syrupy light at golden hour

Changing your space, be it the wall
color, furniture arrangement, or
pen organizer

The pride of making a home
improvement and recognizing
your capabilities.

Cleaning your space and feeling proud
of taking care of yourself

A surprise sale on a product you
needed to buy!

When your furry friend uses you as a
piece of furniture.

Noticing little details on your
neighborhood walk that you can't see
when you drive by

Reminiscing about a favorite memory
with someone you miss

How a furry friend claims a spot as their
own and it becomes forevermore
their spot.

The satisfaction of coloring in a
coloring book.

The excitement of putting color to blank
paper and working without an end goal
in mind.

Seeing two paint strokes meet and blend to create a color of their own

Going for a sip of coffee, expecting it to have gone cold, only to discover it's still lovely and warm and ready to enjoy

Watching humans instinctively move together as music plays

Celebrations of life, joy, growth, and accomplishment

Having someone pick out balloons in your favorite colors because they know you

The confidence of that "Happy Birthday" singer with the high key change solo at the end.

A rocking chair overlooking a pretty view.

Listening to an audiobook and losing yourself in the world of the story

A captivating storyteller

The person in the group who laughs when everyone else ignores the punchline of the joke.

Seeing someone recover after
being unwell

Making the appointment you've
been avoiding

When your favorite artist releases a new
album, so on a drive you listen to the
whole thing from start to finish.

Finding community in a book club,
crafting group, mom's club, and so on

The reassuring smile of a stranger
holding the door open for you even
though you're still far away.

Booking a solo adventure

Someone remembering your
coffee order.

Seeing your friends have babies
and watching them grow

When you find a restaurant that makes
your favorite dish perfectly.

The rehabilitation of an animal.

When you're running late, but so is the
person you're meeting.

How good it feels to chug water when you wake up thirsty in the middle of the night.

How you smile when you are on an airplane, realizing that the patchwork of land beneath you is full of people just like you.

The sense of solidarity that comes from taking a flight—you begin to recognize your fellow passengers and say a soft farewell in your head as they leave the airport terminal.

Wiggling your toes in the morning to wake them up

When you imagine an outfit in your head and it looks exactly how you pictured it.

Buying yourself flowers

The marvelous fact that we have fresh fruit and vegetables available year-round.

Successfully building furniture

The familiarity and comfort of pulling into your street.

Buying the perfect duvet or comforter

When the person directing traffic
returns your wave of thanks.

When you go to check out and find out
that something you bought is on sale
and you hadn't realized.

When your phone easily connects
through Bluetooth.

Driving home after hanging out
with friends

The warmth in your chest when
someone recognizes your hard work.

Someone validating the dream
you have.

Joining a short line only to have it get
very long behind you

Someone letting you merge in traffic.

Looking forward to your lunch because
it's leftovers from a meal you enjoyed the
day before

The feeling of pride after you do
something you've been avoiding.

The privilege of celebrating someone's birthday with them.

Someone remembering your birthday.

How Facebook is today's version of a birthday tracker for your friends and family.

Wondering whether clouds taste like cotton candy or heavy cream

Finding a new favorite song

Seeing your favorite performer live

When someone quotes a movie in
conversation and it happens to be one
of your favorites.

That you haven't had your best day yet.

That you have survived
every challenging day and
difficult season.

Getting a gift card to a store you
really like

How shopping with a gift card feels like
getting things for free

Rubbing your hand over a velvet
pillow—smooth one way,
textured the other

Catching a green light

Catching up to someone at a red light
who sped around you earlier

When someone waves a thank-you
when you let them merge in front
of you.

Someone bringing you home
a piece of cake they sneaked
out for you.

Watching a little kid do a happy dance
when eating something they enjoy

Watching an adult do a happy dance
when eating something they enjoy

Hanging out with a group of people
who all get along

Riding a bike again after you haven't
for a long time

Passing a well-behaved dog in the park

Moms walking with their babies
strapped to their chests.

Befriending a woodland creature near
your home, like stopping to help a turtle
cross the road

Finding a parking space quickly when
you get to somewhere new

Realizing you've gone farther on a walk
than you have before and feeling proud
of yourself for doing something scary
and doing it scared

Catching snippets of strangers'
conversations

Leftover brick outlining a building
of the past.

Strangers joining in when a
table sings "Happy Birthday"
at a restaurant.

Feeling hungry and realizing you
have a snack on hand that'll hold
you over until the next mealtime

The comfort of someone stepping
in to say, "How can I help?"

The nonsensical way mushrooms
grow on stumps.

Finding a photo of a great ancestor
and realizing your dimples came
from them

Getting to the airport with plenty
of time

Riding your bike on a smooth road

Riding your bike down a hill and feeling
like you're flying

Meeting up with a friend you haven't
seen in forever and feeling like no time
has passed

The way babies will close their eyes
while playing hide-and-seek: if they can't
see you, you can't see them.

Feeling reluctant to play board games,
then learning you love the game

Meandering walks and drives with
nowhere to go

The in-between spaces of transition
where your time is your own.

Finding someone who has the
same birthday as you and feeling
inexplicably linked

When you snuggle in bed and finally
find the perfect positioning of blankets
and pillows.

Finding out someone nominated you
for an award that you didn't believe
you were qualified for.

The universal experience of getting your
driver's license and realizing you've
never paid attention to road names
once in your life until now.

Watching a sweet interaction happen
as a bystander and seeing the whole
picture, while each individual could see
only their individual perspective

When everyone slowly waves their
flashlights at a live concert.

When you forget that you put your name on a waitlist for a library book and then get notified that it's ready to be checked out.

Writing with your favorite pen

How the same lunch tastes better when you're out on a picnic than at home.

The way the world's noise becomes fuzzy and then muted as you dunk your head underwater in a bath.

The enveloping stillness of floating on your back

Going barefoot outside, even just for
a minute—feeling the soil, rocks,
sand, grass

Seeing only ripples on the water and
hearing a splash that gives away a turtle
who just spotted you

Seeing a bird's shadow as it
flies overhead

A butterfly zipping through a field.

Tiny minnows swimming in a stream;
once you spot one, you can't stop
seeing them.

Climbing to reach the perfect tree
branch to sit on and read a book

Action movie trailers

The excitement of introducing someone
younger to your favorite book series.

Someone complimenting you in a way
that makes you feel seen.

The curiosity of whether your first
memory is actually a memory or what
your brain has decided to put together
as your first memory.

Introducing two friends you think will get along well

Standing up for yourself. The key is to start small.

Having something in your life that's just your own

The way to build confidence is to just start doing it.

Someone showing you something that they love—a new show, or cooking you their favorite dish.

How life gets a little bit easier as we get older, if for no other reason than we aren't doing everything for the first time anymore.

Finding a perfect spot for an outdoor show

Trying something new and realizing how good it feels to grow

Saying yes to an adventure

Setting up sidewalk chalk drawings for neighborhood kids and watching the adults get in on the hopscotch

Sitting in the car in the driveway after
you get home just for a few moments
of peace for yourself

Train rides

Finishing a book you've started
many times

Slowing down and stopping at a yellow
light instead of pushing to make
it through

Finally remembering to pick up that
item you keep forgetting on the
way home.

The nudge from a furry friend's wet
nose when you stop petting them.

The bravery of trying something new

Collective human excitement

The smell of opening an old book

The overwhelming need to parent the
two squirrels chasing each other.

Learning penny loafers got their name
because they used to have an actual
space for a penny in the front

Coffee outside a street café

Neighbors who let you use their
pool whenever.

A mystery book with an
unexpected twist

The warmth of seeing a loved
one smile.

Taking care of someone you love

Finding someone who likes opposite
flavors of candy than you

The underrated anticipation and excitement you feel before a trip.

A dragonfly hitching a ride on your shoulder up the hill.

Cooking something for the first time and it tasting good

Someone teaching you to blow on a dandelion and make a wish.

The unanimous joy in the air at a concert while hearing your favorite songs live.

The way the leaves flip over with a blast of wind that's a telltale sign of a sudden thunderstorm.

The satisfaction of power washing something

The stump of an old tree becoming a table for fairy tea parties.

A puppy falling asleep while sitting up outside enjoying the sunshine.

The optimism of a dog who sees you holding their favorite toy.

Something being right where you thought it should be.

The smugness that comes from finding something someone else couldn't see right in front of them.

When you try something new to be polite and you wind up liking it.

Friends you can sit in silence with.

A package arriving when it was supposed to.

When someone whose opinion
you respect tells you they're
proud of you.

Rewatching your favorite comfort show
because you know what will happen
and your brain can turn off

A baby's little smile when they're
staring at you over their mother's
shoulder in line.

A server recommending something on
the menu that you would never have
picked, and it becomes your staple
choice every time you eat there.

When you fix something yourself.

When that scary box of instruction
manuals suddenly comes in handy.

The joy of making magic potions
as a kid.

Adults who let children believe in magic.

Going camping and getting to wake
up in nature

The relief of finding out that your
waterproof tent is indeed waterproof.

The helicopter leaves that spin when they fall.

The fact that nature gives us colors we couldn't imagine otherwise.

Someone bringing you a souvenir from their trip to let you know they thought of you while away.

Drawing—creating something where there was nothing

Having someone you love pop into your head

Doing something you thought you could not do

The never-ending debate between pancakes and waffles

When banana bread comes out of the oven and the scent fills the whole house.

Purposely mixing and matching striped and polka-dotted socks

Homemade birthday cakes that look wonky but taste delicious.

Classic rom-com double features

Tucking a child into bed, the blanket
under their chin

When a friend tells you that they saw
something that reminded them of you.

When someone in a group asks what
you were saying after you
were interrupted.

Doing something you were
nervous about and having it go
exceptionally well

Receiving a handwritten letter

Writing a letter by hand

Finding an old favorite stuffed animal
and immediately remembering
their name

Spotting a stranger singing and dancing
in their car

When you crack an egg carelessly but
the yolk still doesn't break.

The phrase, "Say cheese!"

Acknowledgments

To my dad for being our ship and to my mom for being our sails. To Jack for being my first friend and to Joe for being my mirror.

And to everyone who saw me in the darkness and told me there was hope ahead; to the ones who made it through and came back as guides; to those who held space for who I was when I had forgotten it myself. The only way out is through.

About the Author

Emma Jasper was born in the UK and now resides near Washington, DC. She advocates for finding joy in life's small moments, or glimmers, emphasizing that the little things are the big things. With a supportive online community, Emma uses authentic storytelling to invite readers into her own odyssey of vulnerability and profound appreciation. Beyond her literary pursuits, she finds constant joy in the companionship of her two beloved pups.

Follow along at **@thedilemmasofemma** on all platforms.

Rock Point titles are also available at discount for retail, wholesale, promotional, and bulk purchase. For details, contact the Special Sales Manager by email at specialsales@quarto.com or by mail at The Quarto Group, Attn: Special Sales Manager, 100 Cummings Center Suite 265D, Beverly, MA 01915 USA.

10 9 8 7 6 5 4 3 2 1

ISBN: 978-1-57715-481-5

Digital edition published in 2025
eISBN: 978-0-7603-9306-2

Library of Congress Control Number:
2024917973

Group Publisher: Rage Kindelsperger
Editorial Director: Erin Canning
Creative Director: Laura Drew
Senior Art Director: Marisa Kwek
Managing Editor: Cara Donaldson
Editor: Katelynn Abraham
Editorial Assistant: Alyana Nurani
Cover and Interior Design: Maeve Bargman

Printed in China